HALL OF FAITH SERIES

Service and a Smile

NANCY BECK IRLAND

Pacific Press Publishing Association
Boise, Idaho
Oshawa, Ontario, Canada

Edited by Don Mansell
Designed by Consuelo Udave
Cover by Jim Padgett
Type set in 10/12 Century Schoolbook

Library of Congress Cataloging in Publication Data

Irland, Nancy Beck, 1951-
    Service and a smile.

    1. Anderson, Harry, d. 1950. 2. Anderson, Nora. 3. Missionaries—
South Africa—Biography. 4. Missionaries—United States—Biogra-
phy. I. Title.
BV3625.S67175   1987   266'.6732'0922 [B]   87-6902

ISBN 0-8163-0704-0

87 88 89 90 91 ● 5 4 3 2 1

Contents

Chapter 1
Lion Hunt!

"I can see you have not done much tree climbing since you were a boy," Harry muttered wryly to Roscoe Porter as the older man grunted and clawed at the trunk of the tree, one foot wobbling in the palm of Harry's upraised hand.

"I'm afraid I was never too good at shinnying up a tree—especially one whose limbs start this far up," Elder Porter replied with a laugh, wiping his sweaty, red face on his sleeve. He glanced down at the body of a still-warm eland cow, the unfortunate victim of a lion. It was possible that the lion was lurking even now in the tall grass as the men struggled to get up into the highest branches of the tree. They hoped the lion would at least wait until they were out of reach before it came back to its kill. If they were fortunate, they would shoot the lion and take it triumphantly into camp as men who have destroyed the enemy. This was Africa in 1911, and lions *were* the enemy and a continual menace to everyone.

A scorching afternoon sun blazed overhead. Across the dusty, rolling landscape stood an occasional tree among the tall grass. There was no breeze, only the stifling, choking heat.

The day before, young Elder Anderson and his wife had begun their trek with Elder Porter, a visiting minister from the General Conference, to show him some outpost mission stations. They went in what Harry called their car—"not a Cadillac, but a 'cattle-act,'" he called it—two oxen hitched to a wagon with a fabric canopy, much like the covered wagons America's pioneers used crossing the central plains.

The first night out from home, the cattle had been restless.

Harry kept the fires blazing all around the camp for protection from the lions and other wild animals.

Just a few months before, as he was visiting a mission outpost, an African woman had come rushing down the trail toward him, her eyes reflecting horror, as she frantically shouted that her husband and son had just been dragged away by lions. The family had kept fires burning all night long, but as dawn began to break, they felt they were out of danger and had fallen asleep, allowing the fires to burn down. Without their knowing it, hungry lions had crept up on them. The woman had awakened to their screams and watched helplessly as the lions carried them away, dangling lifelessly from their jaws.

Since this terrifying episode Harry had seen the gleaming eyes of lions and other predators watching him in the darkness beyond the crackling fires, sometimes not more than twelve feet away—the distance of a good leap. Their growling and roaring—especially when there were more than one of them—made the earth tremble—as well as the hearts of those huddled within the ring of fire.

"I've learned what the Bible means when it says that Satan walks about like a roaring lion, seeking whom he may devour," Harry said as he stoked the fires around their wagon.

Elder Porter agreed.

"And there's a verse in Zechariah that says God will be like a fire around us to keep us safe," Harry continued. "I reckon, since He made the animals, He knows what He is talking about all right. On one occasion we had to pile thorn bushes around our camp and then light the grass around us so they would burn toward a particularly hungry pack of lions, which were roaring around us, and make them run."

"So the beasts are quite a threat," Elder Porter commented.

"Well, I think that actually only sick or old lions attack humans; but when they decide to attack, they *can* be a threat. But they're mostly curious, I think. If you were to step outside our ring of campfires, you might see their eyes glowing in the darkness even now," Harry said.

"Really?"

"Sure! But don't go too far from the fires; and if you hear a twig snap, run back quickly. Whatever it is, it won't come past the fires," Harry said, smiling confidently at his guest.

The dancing flames cast long shadowy fingers out against the tall grass, and Elder Porter studied them for a long moment before deciding. And then, curious himself, he stepped out of the protective ring of fires a few paces into the dark night.

Harry poked at the fire again with a stick, remembering how it had been when he and Nora had first come to Africa sixteen years before.

At that time Harry was twenty-six, a senior in college, and the Foreign Mission Board asked if he would like to be a missionary. This was early 1895. The year before, 12,000 acres of land had been given to the Seventh-day Adventist Church in southern Africa for a mission school. Harry and Nora were members of a club at Battle Creek College which called itself the "Foreign Mission Band." They were interested in David Livingstone and the growing need for missionaries in foreign lands. They had rejoiced when they heard about the gift of 12,000 acres, thinking it was rich farmland. Though Harry had only been an Adventist for about three years, he already felt a burning desire to share his love for God with others. To think that he was being asked to start a school in the wilds of Africa was a great honor, and Harry felt God had chosen him to go.

"It will be quite an adventure," remarked Elder G. Byron Tripp, who with his family would accompany the Andersons. "The natives are almost entirely devil worshipers. Their witch doctors may try to cast spells on the people you are trying to help.

"Some African customs will be difficult or even impossible for you to understand, and they may not be very pleasant. For example, it is common for the witch doctor to declare that twins, or a baby whose first tooth comes in on the top instead of the bottom, must be killed—usually by exposing them to wild animals or throwing them to the crocodiles. Some of the tribes file their two front teeth into razor-sharp points; others twist their hair into spikes up to three feet long that stick straight up from the tops of their heads.

"And yet, these people need to know about God's love, Harry.

Their lives are filled with fear and sadness because of the evil spirits they worship. Whoever goes must be adventurous and willing to endure hardships."

Harry Anderson was a natural choice. Tall and strong, with the ability to see humor in most situations, he possessed both physical and emotional strength—two essential requirements for a pioneer missionary. Added to this, Nora was a nurse.

Harry considered the call. If he accepted, he would not be able to attend the graduation ceremonies in June. "You see, Harry," Elder Tripp explained, "the last 600 miles of our journey must be made by ox wagon. The rains stop in March or April. If we go later in the year, the streams will be dried up, making the trip impossible."

Nora, his young, pretty wife, encouraged Harry to accept the call to mission service. "You can graduate in absentia," she urged. "Let's go, darling, and share what we know about God's love with those people who don't!"

"I suppose it's not any worse than what Jesus Himself did, leaving a palace to live as a fugitive," Harry said thoughtfully. "It won't be easy for you, Nora. I don't know what sort of accommodations there will be for us. You'll probably not have a lovely home or furniture. And your friends and family—we may not see them again for years. Elder Tripp tells me that there isn't much social life at a mission station. The nationals just don't understand our way of life or our language—" He turned to study her face. "Have you considered all you'd be giving up, Nora?" he asked.

She ran a gentle finger across the length of each of his dark eyebrows. "Don't worry so," she said. "Where God is concerned, we give up something, only to have it replaced by something better." When she saw his gentle smile, she continued, "While we give all, we receive all. We give up our pleasant home, but we receive a mansion prepared for us by Jesus Himself."

"Your family may not understand why I'm taking you so far from home," Harry reminded her. "They may not appreciate the fact that they may never see you again."

"I don't worry so much about having things perfect in this life," Nora replied. "We give a few short years in service, a life which is compared to the life of the grass—it withers soon and dies. What counts is the life we will receive after—a life which measures with the life of God. Things will be perfect then."

"Oh, Nora," Harry said, drawing her small frame into his arms. "If you're sure—"

"I have never been more sure," Nora assured him.

Chapter 2
The Adventure Begins

Their decision made, Harry quickly finished his school-work—three months ahead of schedule—and started preparing for the adventure of his life with Nora, an adventure that would take them halfway around the world to a country where devil worship was a way of life, where insects and wild beasts were a constant threat, and where the white man was often still considered an enemy.

As she shopped and packed for the journey, Nora tried to anticipate all the changes her life would take during the years she would be in Africa. There would be children, of course. Perhaps a daughter. She would need a doll—would Harry let her take a small one? She chose a doll not more than three inches long with beautiful hair and eyes that closed when it was laid down. She couldn't part with her porcelain milk pitcher; it was included, too, along with bolts of fabric, tin plates and cookware, and black stockings for modesty. What if she forgot something? Nora worried.

Harry's purchases were more practical—hoes and axes and carpenter's tools—for they would be farming and building their own house in the middle of wild grassland. There was a shiny stove for Nora, for she did enjoy cooking delightful meals; 12,000 pounds of flour in white, dusty bags; boxes of canned foods from Battle Creek; and heavy gunnysacks filled with cornmeal.

On April 10, 1895, Harry and Nora left for New York City with Elder and Mrs. Tripp and their nine-year-old son, George.

Harry wrote in his diary, "We sailed out of New York harbor on the Steamship *New York,* April 19, and had a very rough, tempestuous voyage of eight days to Southampton [England]. The last three days of the voyage, our baggage was never quiet in the cabin day or night. Our little steamer trunk would first crash across to one side of the cabin, then come back under the berth on the opposite side with a bang, then bound out and hit the door.

"We preferred staying in our berths to [being chased by the] baggage on the floor of the cabin; and not because we were seasick, either. . . ."

When the ship docked at Southampton, all the passengers were herded into a long shed on the docks to pass customs inspection.

Harry and Nora hauled their heavy trunk toward the inspection table as the line moved slowly forward. Then it was finally their turn. Nora looked at Harry nervously and held his gaze for a moment until he flashed her a reassuring smile.

"Baggage up here, please, on this table," the officer said. "Do you have any liquor, cigars, tobacco, or perfumes?" he asked with a tired sigh, as though the question bored him.

Harry's answer was a firm, "No. I have never used liquor or tobacco, sir," he said.

The official leaned over the table and sniffed Harry's breath to satisfy himself that he was telling the truth. Then he scribbled a code on the Anderson's luggage and said they had cleared customs.

Glad to be finished, Harry and Nora dragged their trunk outside over the gray chunks of gravel to wait for the Tripps to get through customs.

After a few delightful days in London, Harry told Nora, "Tomorrow we board our ship, the *Roslin Castle,* for our voyage to Cape Town." He paused a moment before continuing. "I like that name, don't you? *Roslin Castle.*"

"It sounds very luxurious," Nora agreed. "Do you suppose it will be?"

"No doubt," Harry said. "For you, I wouldn't have it any other way."

When Nora looked up at him, he smiled at her warmly and pulled her closer to his side.

Next day they boarded the *Roslin Castle*.

"Oh, Harry, It's so small!" Nora exlaimed in dismay as they climbed the ship's white-painted gangplank. "It's likely to be tossed about like a rubber ball on the sea."

Harry raised his head to look at the two decks towering above them. "Well, it has more than one deck," he said, ever the optimist. "Perhaps someday it will grow into its name and really be a palace."

They stepped onto the first deck and walked through an oval door into a narrow hallway that led to metal stairs. "Our cabin is down," Harry remarked, looking at his ticket.

Nora made a wry face and wrinkled her nose as she carefully raised her skirts and started down the noisy stairs. "What's that smell?" she asked, looking around for the source. "Oil?"

"I think so," returned Harry. When they reached the bottom of the stair, he gestured down the hall and Nora led the way, looking for their cabin number.

"I hope this voyage is not as rough as the one to Southampton," said Nora wrinkling her nose. "This smell could make me sick."

"We'll probably get used to it soon," encouraged Harry. Then, "Oh. Here's our cabin." He opened the white metal door to a long, narrow cabin with room enough for only a bunk bed, a porthole at the end, and a gray, metal sink beneath a small square mirror on the wall.

Nora looked about. It would be very hard to make this cabin into a cozy place; there wasn't anywhere she could lay out her personal things to make it look like home.

"What do you think?" Harry asked with the enthusiasm of a tour guide. He walked over to the porthole and peered out.

"It's very small," Nora said, stepping inside. "Will our voyage be as rough as it was from New York?"

Harry frowned. "Traditionally, the Bay of Biscay, which we'll be passing through, is rather rough sailing," he answered, "but we'll be docking at several ports along the way to Cape Town. If you do get sick, you'll have a stop or two to get your land legs back." With that he shoved a handbag under the bottom bunk.

"How long will it take to get to our first port?" Nora asked as she unpacked her ankle-length dresses and hung them on the peg behind the door.

"About five days, Elder Tripp tells me. That will be Funchal in the Madeira Islands—the 'Pearl of the Atlantic.' "

Nora nodded and raised her eyebrows in a sly smile. "I hope the 'pearl' doesn't prove to be as disappointing as the 'castle,' " she said.

Harry chuckled.

When everything had been stowed away, Harry and Nora stepped through the white oval door into the narrow hall. A wooden handrail snaked above the wooden floor along the white metal walls. Yellow pools of light shone down at regular intervals along the hall, spaced so far apart that Harry and Nora passed through shadow and then light as they found their way to the red metal stairs that led up to the deck.

A burst of fragrant, fresh air blew into their faces as Harry pushed open the heavy oval door to the deck and they stepped over the high threshold.

"We're just in time to watch the departure!" said Harry after the long, ear-splitting blat of the ship's foghorn. The ship slowly glided away from the dock toward the open sea with a swish of churning water, and the Andersons returned the friendly waves of the dock hands at the port.

Chapter 3
On to Africa

Thankfully, the Bay of Biscay did not live up to its reputation for rough seas. The voyage went smoothly, providing the Andersons with memories of moonlit walks along the upper deck. The wind whipped Nora's long, dark skirts about her ankles and pulled thin wisps of hair from the braid she had pinned to the back of her head. Much of their time was spent up at the bow of the ship, leaning on the railing and watching the waves below, laughing at the spray that flew up from time to time when a large swell was split.

In the dining room, they had long discussions with the Tripps about their expectations of Africa, and the two families soon became close friends.

Cape Town was a city of 67,000 inhabitants, with 70,000 more in the suburbs on the peninsula. It boasted beautiful public gardens, a museum and art gallery, and an old castle with large guns for protection. It was a beautiful city with a warm, balmy breeze blowing in from the ocean. It seemed quite modern to the Andersons and consisted of a mixture of English, Dutch, Greek, Malay, and African cultures.

After a scenic tour of the city in the afternoon, the Andersons and the Tripps found their way to the train station for the next leg of their journey. They were met there by a Dr. A. S. Carmichael, 55 years old, from California. He would be the mission doctor. Because he was the oldest of the missionaries, he would become like a father to them.

"Where's the ticket office?" Harry asked after formal introductions were over.

Dr. Carmichael pointed to a small enclosed cubicle at the center of the station. "I've been here about half an hour, and that's the only office I've seen," he said. "It says 'booking office.' That must be the same thing."

"Well, I guess in Africa we get our 'bookings' rather than our 'tickets,' " Harry said, chuckling. "Shall we go?" They walked to the small enclosure.

"Are you the booking agent?" Harry asked the man behind the window.

"The booking *clerk*," the man replied, pronouncing *clerk* as *clark*. "Where are you going?"

"To Mafeking," Elder Tripp said.

"That's the end of the line," the clerk told them.

"Yes, I know." Elder Tripp turned to talk quietly to Harry and Dr. Carmichael. "We'll go to the end of the line, and then we'll take oxcarts to the mission acreage."

Harry nodded.

The booking clerk slipped their tickets under the window and pointed out the platform where the train was waiting.

Africa had three classes of railway coaches. The first class was nicely upholstered with a window for each seat. The second-class coaches consisted of eight separate compartments in one coach that opened onto a narrow hall. Third class was just behind the engine. The seats there were just bare boards, with no upholstery.

The mission group had been advised to travel second-class coach. They found their compartment, a small one, about seven feet square. Each compartment slept six people, the beds being the two bench seats on either side of the window, the backs of the benches that could be raised and fastened to chains dangling from the ceiling, and two more berths up against the ceiling, fastened with chains, that could be let down.

Some of the luggage was shipped by freight, but 23 pieces of it were stored on the two upper berths, and the five adult missionaries plus young George Tripp sat shoulder to shoulder on the bottom benches.

The conductor came. After checking their tickets and finding that they were riding to the end of the line, he locked the door of their compartment—"So you can travel in safety," he explained.

Nora twisted apprehensively and ran a hand across her sweaty forehead. She looked up at Harry, who squeezed her hand reassuringly and smiled at her. It made her feel a little better.

As the clock on the station tower chimed eight o'clock that evening, the train gave a lurch; the cars bumped against each other; the shrill whistle blew; and they were on their way. A cool breeze blew in the window. Though it was dark outside, George leaned against the windowsill, his chin cupped in his hand, and watched what he could of the passing scenery with the excitement of a child.

As the train moved slowly out of Cape Town toward the northeast, the missionaries missed seeing the most beautiful part of their trip: long stretches of sandy, yellow soil on which many grapevines and strawberry patches were growing. From there, the train headed up into the hills, passing a giant black rock known as the Pearl. Beyond that lay miles of orange and lemon groves with fragrant blossoms and waxy leaves. Up and up into the mountains the little train chugged along, throwing red-hot cinders from the smokestack into the windows.

The rails clicked off the miles in a steady rhythm, coming down from the mountains onto the interior plateau, called the Karroo, a desolate-looking region covered with sagebrush. Here the Dutch had large farms for raising angora goats, fat-tailed sheep, and ostriches.

Around midnight, under a silver moon, the train passed by open diamond mines, then entered the fertile grazing district around Mafeking. The missionaries slept fitfully, cool at last, leaning their bobbing heads against each others' shoulders. The train slowed, at last, very early in the morning near the town of Mafeking, and with a final lurch, it came to a squeaky stop at a small siding. The passengers slept restlessly in the darkness, until the windows of their compartments were light gray squares in the quiet dawn.

"Nora," Harry called softly, giving her a gentle nudge. "Nora. We're here."

While Dr. Carmichael stayed with George and the women, Harry and Elder Tripp walked a short distance into town to find the ox-drawn wagons the workers in Cape Town had bought for them. They learned, in dismay, that the total cost of the wagons and oxen had exhausted their allotted funds for their first year at the school.

"We'll have to be self-supporting now," Elder Tripp announced.

"Perhaps we can sell one or two of the wagons once we get there and get some of our money back," Harry suggested.

They sent a local boy back to the train station with a cart drawn by four oxen. As the oxen neared the train, they suddenly bolted away wild-eyed, white, frothy saliva dripping from their mouths.

Nora and Mrs. Tripp watched with wide eyes as the boy raced after the cart. It took some time for him to get the oxen settled down and back to the train. By that time Harry and Byron arrived at the train station with the two wagons drawn by 14 oxen each. They were joined by Mr. and Mrs. Fred Sparrow and their two young sons. The Sparrows were missionaries with experience in farming. They were familiar with the trails to the school property and the town of Bulawayo, thirty-two miles beyond. Bulawayo was the seat of government in Rhodesia, and fairly modern.

Harry was concerned about Nora's comfort during the long trek that lay ahead of them. "You ladies can ride in the cart with George," he suggested, "so you don't have to walk the whole way."

"Thank you, but I think I'd rather let the *luggage* ride with those unpredictable beasts," Nora responded with a nervous chuckle "I trust my own legs more than I do theirs."

"Well, maybe if I drive them instead of the boy, they will behave," Harry suggested.

By the time they were ready to leave that afternoon, Harry had talked the women into riding in the cart, certain that the animals would be calmer with him driving them.

With a reassuring smile in Harry's direction, Nora gathered up her skirts, took his outstretched hand, and climbed up into the cart.

"When you get sleepy, you can rest in the bed I made in the wagon," Harry informed her. He had placed a spring mattress on top of the boxes of Battle Creek foods. The wagon covering came over the top, making a cozy little place for them to sleep.

"You can't sit up in it," Harry had said.

"That's OK—I prefer to sleep lying down," Nora had said with a smile.

Dr. Carmichael would sleep in the front of the wagon. The Tripps had made a bed on top of the flour sacks, rather lumpy, to say the least, but at least it was a place to lay their heads.

They would drive until night fell and then sleep within the protection of bonfires until three or four o'clock in the morning, when they would resume their journey. Four or five hours later they would stop for breakfast and make camp until the heat of the day had passed, then start again around two o'clock in the afternoon.

"I'll drive the oxen the first part," Harry offered. "After watching how that boy drove them, I'm sure I can do better— I'm fresh out of college, after all, and fairly bursting with knowledge! If a native boy can drive the 14 oxen of the wagon just in front of me, I can certainly drive four alone." But he soon wished he had not been so self-confident.

Chapter 4
Runaway Wagon!

"Fall in!" Fred Sparrow called, and the first wagon started down the trail.

Harry smiled, feeling a little like an American pioneer crossing the plains. Standing beside the cart, he adjusted his hat and cracked his whip over the heads of the oxen. Nobody expected what happened next. With a start, the four strong oxen bolted, hauling the cart as fast they could go across the plain.

"Harry! Do something!" Nora cried as she was carried off on the runaway cart toward the wilderness. She and Mrs. Tripp bounced violently about, helplessly screaming at the top of their lungs.

Harry ran after the team as fast as his legs would carry him, shouting and cracking his whip. When the oxen turned and started toward the other wagons, Harry caught up to them. He was just about to head them into the road when he plunged into a thorn tree, known by the Dutch as "wait-a-bit." The thorn is shaped like a fishhook, barb and all. And Harry did wait quite a bit as he extracted himself with difficulty from the vicious thorns, donating a section of one of his trouser legs in the process.

The oxen, however, had missed the thorn bush and kept on running.

Finally, tattered and torn, Harry caught up with the cart and turned the oxen back to the road. They continued to run wildly, and very soon they locked wheels with the wagon in front. This brought the whole wagon train to a grinding halt.

With his tattered trousers and grimy face, Harry looked as

though he had been wandering the desert for months.

"Oh, Harry, are you all right?" Nora called down when she saw him.

Harry nodded, his sides heaving, and wiped perspiration from his forehead with what remained of his sleeve. "I'll be fine now," he said, panting. "How are *you* doing?"

"A little shaken—in more ways than one—but I'll be OK. Do you want someone else to drive?" Nora asked.

"Whatever for?" Harry asked defensively. "I'll do fine—" now that the oxen are tired and a little more manageable, he added to himself. Obediently, the team fell into line behind the other wagons and Harry looked up and smiled confidently at Nora as they resumed their journey the way it should have been from the beginning. "They just had to learn who was boss," Harry muttered smugly.

"So you've met the 'wait-a-bit' tree," Fred twitted that night when they had made their camp, forming a circle with the wagons and the cart and lighting fires around them. Fred continued: "The group that traveled this same route last year had quite a humorous experience. One of the men was traveling on top of the load, asleep, when the wagon passed under the low branches of a particularly vicious wait-a-bit tree. Some of the thorns brushed over his sleeping form and fixed themselves in the strong khaki clothing he was wearing."

"Oh, no," Harry groaned, imaging the rest of the story.

Mr. Sparrow nodded. "Yup! The wagon passed on, but the man remained suspended in midair. Suddenly awakening and finding himself a living hammock, the man stared down at the road beneath him and shouted for help. We thought his predicament was humorous, but he didn't think so. It took quite a while to set him free without totally ruining his clothing."

Harry chuckled. "I guess I was lucky, then," he said. "All I left behind was a bit of my trousers and sleeve."

Each day that the group traveled seemed the same. There was little change in the scenery.

"It's scrub brush, thorns, and grass, and then thorns, grass, and scrub brush," Harry observed as they bounced along in the early morning quietness. Only the crunch of the wooden wheels on an occasional stone, the steady rhythm of the oxen's hooves pounding the packed earth, and the creaking and squeaking of the wagons broke the monotony. From time to time large herds of antelope would thunder across the plain in fright as the wagons approached. In the distance, a troop of long-necked giraffes nibbled at the top leaves of the trees.

"We don't seem to be making much progress," Harry commented one day. "We've been traveling for three days already, and have covered only ten miles."

Nora patted his knee. "They warned us it would be tedious," she replied, "but actually the scenery from the ship was more monotonous. I'm getting more sick of our meals than of the scenery. I wish I could cook something besides graham mush, and serve it with crackers, and cereal coffee for breakfast every morning." She thought a moment. "Perhaps I can cook something special for supper tonight. How does fresh bread sound?"

"If that's the carrot hanging under my nose, I'll keep going," Harry returned with a tired smile.

The strains of a song floated on the air from the Sparrows' wagon. "Let us sing a song that will cheer us on our way, in a little while we're going home."

Nora began to hum, and soon she and Harry were singing and smiling together, barely noticing the unchanging landscape, the scorching sun, and the dry, searing heat.

When they stopped, Nora hurried for some flour and the iron baking pots. "I promised Harry I would bake some bread for him," she explained to Mrs. Tripp. "Can you help me?"

The women served the fresh bread at supper with pride. "Well, what do you think?" Nora asked, studying Harry's face carefully. He was gnawing on a corner of his loaf.

"I'm sure it's very tasty," Harry said, "but I'm afraid my jaw is not strong enough to bite it off or chew it." He winked at his pretty wife.

"Too tough?" Nora asked in dismay.

"Don't give up," Harry said then, seeing he had hurt her feelings. "I'm sure it is much different cooking over a campfire like this than it was at home."

"Do you think so?" Nora asked, feigning surprise. And then the sight of Harry gnawing on his loaf like a hungry dog made her chuckle. Soon the entire group around the fire was laughing together.

About four o'clock one morning, the group came to a portion of the road that was made entirely of stones. Harry happened to be sleeping at the time, and he wrote later in his diary: "Those of our company who remained in bed heartily wished they were up. Perhaps you can imagine how it would be to lie in a spring bed mounted on boxes, and every time the wagon went over a stone, to strike first the box beneath and then the wagon cover above."

Four days after leaving Mafeking the little band of missionaries found themselves among the mountains. Now the road wound around the hills and over the rocks. Their progress was even slower than before.

When Sabbath came, the group stopped for the day. Dr. Carmichael went into a nearby village to offer medical treatment. He found a band of Christians there who pleaded with him to stay and work with them. "The Matebele tribe you will be living near at your mission are cruel and bloodthirsty," they said. But Dr. Carmichael answered that they could not stay.

That evening they had planned to move on, but Fred was feeling ill, so they stayed in camp. One extra day stretched to five. Although the missionaries were all convinced that a vegetarian diet was best for them, yet they were concerned that their bread-only meals were not complete. So, they agreed that until they got settled, they would add meat to their diet to avoid illness. Harry and Byron spent their time in the mountains hunting antelope, which roamed the mountains in large herds. Each evening it was the same.

"Did you catch anything?" the women would ask.

And Harry would explain patiently, with mock surprise, "No, somehow my gun didn't shoot straight today!" He would study the gun in amazement and shake his head.

Fortunately, one of the African drivers returned from his own hunting trip one day with an antelope, which he shared with the group.

On June 13, after their long break, the group began traveling again as soon as it was daylight and soon came to a river with very steep banks. Byron went ahead to test the current and see the wagons safely across, and then came back to help Harry with the cart. Since there was no brake on the cart, the men had to do the braking! Taking hold of the back part of the cart and bracing their feet, they skidded down to the water's edge, red dust flying out behind them. When the wild-eyed oxen splashed into the water, their heads barely above the water, the men sprang into the cart and rode across the river.

On June 16, the little wagon train began what would be one of their longest continuous treks. They had to pass from one river to another, a distance of nearly forty miles, without water. The situation was potentially dangerous, as the oxen, as well as the people, needed water desperately every evening to make up for the fluids they lost because of the heat. They would have to make the trek of forty miles as fast as they could go.

They traveled from three until eight o'clock in the morning, and then stopped to rest. After only five hours of traveling, the oxen already wanted to drink. So the native drivers, without a note of protest, led the oxen back eight miles to the river without their loads. The trip there and back took all day, and at three-thirty that afternoon the oxen were hitched to the wagons and the pressing pace continued.

The missionaries kept up an exhausting schedule during the rest of the afternoon, through the night, and until noon the next day, alternately driving and resting—driving four hours and resting two. At the midnight rest, Harry lay down by the fire to get a short nap. "But," as he later wrote in his diary, "I was soon brought back from the land of nod by a burning sensation and found that my trousers were afire." Luckily he awakened before either he or his clothing sustained serious damage.

Chapter 5
A Hut for a Home

The next day the group stopped near a native village and were welcomed warmly by the villagers. They surrounded the wagons with smiling faces. And when they smiled, Nora noticed that their front teeth had been filed into razor-sharp points. Their earlobes, stretched out of shape by weights, brushed against their shoulders. The chief's earlobes were not so long, just the right size to hold a yellow pencil, which hit against his cheeks when he shook his head.

Fred translated what the chief was saying. His village had heard of Christian missionaries and asked that one of this group stay and teach them more. Sadly, Fred had to tell him that they had another assignment.

"I wonder if God's own sadness is not even greater than ours, that there are not enough missionaries to go everywhere there is a need," Harry mused.

On June 18, 1895, Harry remembered with a touch of sadness that his friends were graduating from college that day. "And *my* commencement exercises consist of driving an ox wagon in Africa!" he commented.

The trekkers stopped near another native village to ask for water. This tribe evidently identified themselves by pulling out their front teeth. None of the villagers Harry saw had any. Fred confirmed this conclusion. The adults held the young people down when it was time to mark them and yanked out their front teeth amid much screaming and writhing. It helped them know at a glance, should the tribes fight, who was one of them and who was not.

27

The chief of the village told them that the oxen could graze down at a river about seven miles away.

"Is that the closest water?" Harry wondered.

Fred listened to the chief for several minutes, then said, "There's a well just a short ways down that trail." He pointed in the direction the chief had indicated. "We can get water for our entire group there."

"Thank you," Harry said. He looked at Byron. "Shall we take some buckets and bring the water back for the ladies?" And he agreed.

When the men arrived at the "well," they were surprised to find it was just a shallow depression in the earth, like a bowl. Worse still, a woman was washing her feet in the water! They asked her to kindly finish, then, after waiting until the water cleared, they dipped all the water out and sat down to wait for more to well up.

After about two hours there was almost enough water to fill one bucket. With that single bucket they would have to do all their cooking and washing for one day. "For some reason, the rice we cooked that day turned black," Harry wrote in his diary, "but we were hungry, and enjoyed it just the same."

At their next stop, the missionaries were happily surprised to find a well with a hand pump. They pumped water for the oxen, but the animals would not drink from the wooden trough, even though they were thirsty. They simply refused to touch the water.

"I imagine they have never had water from a trough before," Fred suggested.

Harry ran a frustrated hand through his hair and pondered what they could do to encourage the oxen to drink. Byron had an idea. He and Harry dug a trench, lined it with a strip of canvas, and carefully covered the edges with dirt. Then they carried water and filled the trench. When the oxen were brought up, they drank greedily.

As the weary party traveled along through the differing areas of landscapes, they asked Fred how Solusi got its name and what it was like.

"Solusi is the name of a friendly chief who lives not far from the acreage," Fred explained. "And as to what the acreage is like, it's like everything we have gone through."

Harry wrote a frustrated entry in his diary one night: "When we came through Bechuanaland (now Botswana) which was dry and sandy, he [Fred] told us the mission farm was like that; and our hearts sank. When we came to another section of country, which was fairly well timbered with scrub trees, he told us the mission farm was like that; and as we entered the Matopo Hills and saw the massive heaps of rock on every hand, he told us the mission farm was like that."

At last, on July 26, 1895, after six weeks of camping out, Fred announced that they were on the mission farm! Up ahead they saw four mud huts, built by the local people for them. The huts were surprisingly inviting.

Harry drove into the settlement and drew in the oxen. He helped Nora off the wagon. After appropriate words of excitement, she clapped her hands together, then crawled through the two-and-a-half foot high door into the hut.

"It's cool in here!" she called excitedly, and the other families crawled into their huts to see for themselves.

The huts were about fourteen feet wide with walls five feet high and rounded roofs covered with a thin coat of grass. The local Africans, being shorter, could stand up in the very center. But at least it was home. Harry's first thought was that the grass roofs would never keep out the monsoon rains which would come in October. He started planning a better shelter for Nora.

As he wandered among some of the 12,000-acre tract, he kept looking for suitable trees with which to build a log house. He had been told that the area was "heavily timbered" and was surprised there weren't more suitable trees. But he soon learned that while there were not a lot of trees, the only ones around were *heavy*—so heavy they wouldn't float. There were many tall bushes. On one occasion Harry had to climb a tree to see over them and find his way back to the settlement.

The acreage was beautiful, though, and the view was extensive and diversified, just like Fred told them it would be, with hills and valleys and an abundant growth of vegetation.

"If this farm were in a city it would be regarded as a natural park," Harry wrote in his diary. "It is very picturesque, with a great variety of flowers and grass, many species of trees, and two varieties of mammoth cactus. Massive granite boulders, many of them delicately poised, look as if the slightest touch would send them rolling to the bottom of the hills which they crown. Unfortunately a farmer doesn't especially like to see his farm covered with them."

On reaching the mission station it seemed that everything had to be done at once. The garden must be planted immediately, houses built, trading with the natives carried on, sewing done to clothe the local women, and a well dug, besides much other work incident to pioneer life.

In selecting a site for the garden, Harry went about three fourths of a mile away where he found some very wet land. When he had plowed about half of it, the soil became so wet that the furrow he was making filled up with water, and the oxen began to mire down, so he had to stop. In spite of this, the garden started growing nicely before long, and they hired Africans to begin clearing the land near the house.

They began living as comfortably as they could in their huts, but after the garden was planted and they had set the workers to clearing the land, Harry and Byron decided to find poles for building some temporary houses.

The trees in that area are usually crooked, gnarled, and twisted, and the men discovered that it was difficult to find poles eight feet long that were anywhere near straight. Eventually, however, they found enough.

One day when Harry was going through the woods with a local boy, he discovered a clump of very nice, straight poles, from which he thought he could get some good rafters. In his broken English the boy tried to urge Harry not to cut them. He said, "One month, good; two month, good; three month, no good."

Harry failed to understand his explanation, so he cut one of the best poles and put it into his hut for a rafter. To his dismay, Harry found that it was just as the boy had said—one month, good; two months, good; but the third month, the pole broke because the wood borers had honeycombed it—practically eaten it up.

"I learned," Harry told Nora that evening, "that although I came to Africa to teach the natives, there are many things they can teach *me*."

One day as Nora was going about her work in the hut with the usual audience of a half dozen or more women sitting outside the door, they caught sight of her black stockings above the tops of her shoes. They all jumped up, clapped their hands, and shouted in their own language, "She is black! She is black, just like the rest of us! It is only her face that is white!"

One thing the women couldn't understand was why Nora didn't have any children. Mrs. Tripp had George, of course, and Mrs. Sparrow had two young sons and was expecting another baby in January; but Nora was childless. In the villagers' eyes this was a disgrace. Nora did not know how to explain that she did not consider it a problem.

One day, as they were asking the usual question, Nora remembered the doll she had packed away before she sailed for Africa. She went to her trunk, brought out the doll, and showed it to the women.

"This is my only baby," she said with a smile, showing the fascinated women how the doll's eyes closed when she laid it down and opened when it was held upright. The women beheld the doll in awe, jabbering to each other seriously. Very soon, the fame of that doll went out through the country. Women and children would sometimes walk fifteen or twenty miles to see the baby that was kept in a box, never cried, and would close its eyes and go to sleep at once when it was laid down. And when they asked, Nora patiently showed it to them with a smile.

Dr. Carmichael met with distressing superstitions in the villages. It was a common practice for the people to plunge their arms into a vat of boiling water to prove whether or not they were lying about any incident in question. If their arm blistered, they were considered liars; if they came through the ordeal without blisters, it was believed that they had told the truth. If anyone questioned whether or not they were lying, even the children would say, wide-eyed, "I'll stick my arm in boiling water!"

Because of the filthy conditions in the villages, many of the blistered arms became infected. But while most of the villagers took their medical problems to the local witch doctor, a few allowed Dr. Carmichael to treat them. In time, his medicines became more trusted, and the people around the mission were eager to try any medicine the white doctor offered them.

The calendar said October when the men started cutting down trees to build houses. Already they had built a church, dug a well, cleared thirty acres of land, planted a thriving garden, and had begun to learn the language from the people. The natives of the surrounding area attended church out of curiosity, wearing clothes the missionaries helped them make. Some of the men wore their shirts in a way all their own, with their legs in the arms of the shirt and the rest of the shirt tied around their waists. The women tied tubes of calico fabric around themselves, leaving their shoulders bare.

Most of Harry's time was spent working on his house, filling in the gaps between the crooked poles with thick mud. It was tedious, backbreaking work. If he finished in time, Harry hoped there would be enough hot days to dry the mud completely before the monsoon rains came. And if not—He didn't want to think of what the wet mud would do in the rain.

Harry wanted to put down a smooth, polished wood floor for Nora, but the planks he priced in Bulawayo were too expensive. But even if they had had the money, a wood floor was not practical, for wood borers would have quickly eaten it up.

"The local people use cow dung for their floors," Fred suggested one day as they worked together on Harry's house. He smiled wryly.

"And I suppose there is plenty of that around," Harry agreed, looking over at the oxen. "But I'm not sure Nora would be proud of a cow-dung floor!"

"Then I guess you'll have to put up with a plain dirt floor, my friend," Fred replied.

"Well, at least it's *clean*," Harry muttered to himself.

Window coverings were Harry's next concern. Because mosquitoes carried malaria, he wanted to keep as many of them out of the house as possible. First he fastened mosquito netting over the window; but the white ants ate it up. Then he got more netting and covered the bed with it; but the white ants ate that up too. At last he gave up, frustrated, hoping that if the malaria came, they could take quinine and beat it.

The house was finished the first week in November. Harry brought in Nora's stove proudly and set it up carefully in the corner of the kitchen. He had to construct a stove pipe out of tin cans to extend the one that came with the stove because the ceiling was so high, but everything came together beautifully.

That evening, by the light of kerosene lanterns, Nora polished the stove carefully, as she planned breakfast for the next morning—the first time in six months she would not be cooking over a smoky campfire! Being a missionary hadn't proved to be *that* unpleasant, she thought to herself. And it certainly was never dull. Beginning tomorrow, they would have fresh bread and biscuits and scrambled eggs—all cooked on a real stove!

It was late by the time Harry pried Nora from her stove and talked her into going to bed. "You'll want to be rested for your baking tomorrow," he said.

Before long, the Andersons awakened to the sound of rain—heavy rain that beat down on the roof of the house and peppered the still-damp walls without mercy. Steady streams of water poured down through the roof. Harry opened up their umbrellas to keep their heads dry. Nora pulled the covers up around her and closed her eyes, not wanting to see if the walls were sliding away. Somehow she went back to sleep until the first light of day crept into the room through the gray square that was the window.

Harry was up first. He swung his feet over the side of the bed and was instantly awake when they landed in wet, soggy mud! "Wonderful," he muttered to himself. Mud squished up between his toes and was soon cold around his ankles as he sloshed into the kitchen, where his low groan brought Nora at once to his side. The walls had caved in, piling eight inches of mud on top of her brand new stove!

Speechless, Nora turned to Harry and buried her face in his shoulder. For the first time in the six months since they left America, she cried.

Harry did what he could to comfort her, and she soon dried her eyes and set about cleaning up the place.

Chapter 6
Trying Days

The next week, Nora and Mrs. Tripp went to one of the villages close by for the wedding of one of the village boys who had been working for them. It was Nora's first visit to a native village. She was appalled at the condition in which the people lived. In order to protect themselves from wild animals, the village was surrounded by poles and thorn bushes. Inside this fence, all the huts making up the village were arranged in a circle, with the small round doors—only thirty inches high— facing into the circle. The chief's house was almost always situated on the far side of the village, away from the main entrance, with the houses of his wives on either side.

The whole inner courtyard of the village was the cattle corral. Some villages had room for only fifty cows in this corral. The larger villages sometimes held up to 2,000 cows, which roamed around between the huts. Sheep, goats, chickens, and dogs wandered about in the corral during the day, then were taken inside the stuffy huts at night to sleep with the family. Since there were no windows in the huts, and since the people rarely bathed, the odor inside was overwhelming.

If this was bad, it was far worse in the rainy season, when the mud in the corral was often knee-deep—a mixture of mud and animal manure. Mr. Sparrow explained that sometimes when the missionaries visited the villages they would be carried on the back of one of the men and poles were laid across the threshold to the hut on which they could stand.

"That's OK, as long as the villager doesn't stumble and dump me into the mud," Harry commented wryly.

Fortunately, the rainy season had just begun, so the mud was not too deep, and the wedding ceremony was celebrated with the usual feasting and dancing. At the close of the day, the villagers, according to their custom, accompanied the missionaries a little distance along the path.

When they parted, Chaba Chaba, the head man of the party, took Mrs. Tripp by the shoulders and gave her a goodbye kiss, as he had seen the missionary men do. Surprised, and not wishing for a repeat performance on her, Nora made her escape by running down the trail as fast as she could go. Mrs. Tripp caught up with her shortly and said the chief was just trying to do what he thought was considered good manners in America.

"Perhaps he was," Nora laughed, "but I prefer to save my kisses for my husband."

Because of the heavy rains, the corn flourished. The Africans marveled at the abundance of healthy plants and asked what the missionaries used for medicine to make their gardens grow so well. Harry pointed to the sweat on his brow. "This is what does it," he said.

One afternoon, the Andersons, the Tripps, the Sparrows, and Dr. Carmichael were having a Bible study among themselves when they noticed the sunlight outside was suddenly gone. When they went outside, the sky was darkened by a thick cloud of locusts. The missionaries watched helplessly, not knowing what to do to protect their garden. Less than half an hour later there was not a trace of green anywhere.

"It's gone!" Nora cried in disbelief. "The corn is gone!"

"Now what do we do?" Mrs. Tripp asked. It was a question no one wanted to think about. If their garden didn't grow, they would have no food—no food to eat, none to sell, no money for their needs.

"We can replant the corn," said Fred, "and it can be harvested before the dry season comes. But the beans—"

Harry took off his hat and scratched his head. His eyes wore a pained expression.

"The beans are lost," Byron said with finality.

"Well, at least we'll have corn," said Nora optimistically, looking around the group.

"And if the locusts come again—what then?" Mrs. Tripp asked with a worried frown.

"If the locusts come again, after the corn is replanted," suggested Fred, "we can gather all the helpers possible and go into the cornfield with tin cans and run up and down the rows, beating the tin cans and throwing dirt on the pests to scare them off. Or we can dig trenches between the rows and brush them off the plants and into the ditches and then bury them alive."

Nora shuddered.

"You know," Fred continued, "locusts never turn back. So, once they are driven through the fields too fast to eat, they just keep on going."

"If that is true, I hope they never return," Mrs. Tripp said firmly, clasping her hands tightly in her lap and fixing her mouth in a tight line.

"Now, if we ate them, as the natives do," Fred laughed, "we would *welcome* the locusts rather than resent their appearance."

Chapter 7
The Matabele Uprising

As if the locust plague was not enough, the cattle began dying of a disease called rinderpest, and those that lived were quarantined. Without the oxen to pull the plows, gardening became very difficult.

Harry feared for the future of the mission. In December 1895, rumors began circulating that the leader of the British South African Company, which ruled Rhodesia (now Zimbabwe), had tried to overthrow the government of the South African republic, and Harry worried about war. The fierce Matabeles were angry. They were ruthless and would do anything to show their anger.

The Englishman who was causing trouble was captured, and his entire army—the police force of Rhodesia—were taken prisoner. This left the country, where the mission was located, without a ruler and without a police force to protect it.

The Matabeles persuaded the other tribes not to trust England as a military power. They suggested that all white people were dishonest and should be killed or run out of the country.

In January of 1896, Umlevu, the head chief in the area where the mission farm was located, came to Byron and told him that the Africans were going to rebel. In two moons they would begin to fight the English. Byron tried to talk them out of fighting, explaining that even if they killed all the white people in Africa, there were still many more left in England to come and fight. Umlevu agreed that they would not fight the missionaries, but he was determined to rebel against the English rule.

Two months later, Byron was pacing the floor in Harry's home, when he said, "It's March, Harry. It's been two moons since Umlevu was here. Remember, the fighting was going to begin in two moons."

"What shall we do?" Harry asked.

"I don't want the women to be frightened until we know more," said Byron. "Mrs. Sparrow has those two young sons and just had her baby girl. She certainly doesn't need anything more to worry about. But I don't like being in the dark about this! I think I should walk in to Bulawayo to see if there is any talk about an uprising, and then, if necessary, we can plan our escape better."

"Right!" Harry agreed. "God be with you, brother."

When Byron returned, the only thing he knew was that the English leaders had angered the Africans by sending messengers to ask the native chiefs to come into town for counsel. Only one chief had responded, and he had been promptly arrested and thrown into jail.

"That could be the only incident the other chiefs need, to rebel," Byron worried. "And I can't say that I would trust the white man, either, if they double-crossed one of my people."

The next week, Harry went to town on business. Since all the cows were quarantined, he could only go on foot—thirty-two miles! He left at three o'clock in the morning with two native boys he had never met before. They arrived in town six hours later, at nine o'clock in the morning.

Harry went to the market and quickly sold the butter and eggs he had brought. As he started down the street to complete the rest of his business, he saw a man galloping up Seventh Avenue, his horse covered with foam. He was shouting, "The Matabeles have risen and are massacring everybody in the district!"

Harry's heart lurched. He wondered if the massacres were confined to that district, or if the natives were killing all white men anywhere. What about Nora? And the others? Could they have been massacred already? Suddenly feeling the uncertainty that comes with war, Harry wasn't sure what the two native boys who had accompanied him might do on their way back to the mission. They could kill him.

Harry's first priority was to go to the government headquarters and find out as much as he could. Then he told the native boys to go back to the mission by the wagon road with the supplies he had bought. It was Harry's plan to take a shortcut back to the mission and arrive there before the boys did, just in case they planned a massacre of their own.

Later that day, as Harry turned his steps homeward his stomach growled and knotted with hunger. His feet burned from the heat of the packed earth of the trail. He longed for a drink, but there were no springs nearby, and besides, stopping might make him vulnerable to the wild animals. The tropical sun vanished like a snuffed candle, and the air became cool.

Fighting the overwhelming pleas of his body for rest, Harry pushed on, running and then walking, peering into the grasses and bushes along the side of the path for wild animals who might be lurking there. The muscles in his legs felt like twisted ropes. It seemed he would never arrive! But at last he saw the sleeping settlement ahead of him, and he breathed a prayer of thanks that buildings were untouched. It was two o'clock in the morning, just a little less than twenty-four hours since he had left there. He stumbled in the moonlight toward his house.

As a precaution against being ambushed by natives who might be hiding in his house, Harry crept to the bedroom window and called Nora's name. When he heard her voice, he hurried inside. Nora was safe.

Waking the Tripps immediately, the missionaries held a middle-of-the-night discussion and decided to leave right away; the situation was extremely grave.

Before the sun was up, everyone was packing at a frantic pace, boxing up books, bedding, and food to take with them. They wished they could save everything, but having sold all but one wagon, it was impossible to load all the things for four families into it. With a last quick goodbye to her stove, Nora silently watched the men bury it in a deep hole, along with her dishes and other things which the white ants could not devour.

Word went out that the missionaries were offering bargains on everything in their store, and the villagers came early in the morning and bought nearly everything that was there. The cattle in quarantine were left in the care of the local people.

"Who will protect us while you're gone?" the Africans asked in dismay. But Harry did not know what to say. "Just don't take part in the rebellion," he pleaded.

That evening, sixteen hours after Harry had arrived home, the little band of five missionaries set out for Bulawayo, pulling their wagon themselves. They passed the two native boys Harry had sent home on the road the day before.

The second day of their travel to Bulawayo, the missionaries camped beside the Khami River. The women and children slept, but the men stayed up to guard the camp against any one who might come to harm them.

Crickets chirped all night. There were no other sounds until just before daybreak. One of the men heard a shrill call like that of a night bird up the river. It was immediately answered by a similar cry from down the river and then from down the ridge at the back of their camp. They knew it was the call of the Matabeles, preparing for an attack on their camp.

Everyone was awakened. Fires were started around the camp so that the attackers would have to reveal themselves in the light before they could see any of the white men.

The missionaries waited anxiously, ready to protect themselves; but the Matabeles became suddenly quiet and did not attack. They learned later that a few days before, this same group had killed a man sleeping under his wagon, stolen his oxen and all his goods, and then burned the wagon and his dead body in order to hide the evidence.

After a harrowing journey, the tired group of missionaries arrived in Bulawayo. They were running out of money, and to rent a room or a house in town was more than they could afford. So they found a spot in the corner of the hospital grounds on the outskirts of town and decided to live in their wagon as long as possible.

A curtain divided the wagon into two compartments. The Sparrows, including their young sons and their six-week old daughter, Amy, had their bed in the front "room;" the Tripps made their home in the back "room," with George sleeping underneath their bed. Harry and Nora slept under the wagon.

When they had been there about two weeks, Nora awakened Harry in the middle of the night.

"Harry, it's raining!" she exclaimed in a loud whisper.

"Yes, it is," he replied groggily.

"Well, let's get up," Nora said.

"Up where?" Harry groaned. There was no place for them to go. Their bed was so placed that the rain from the cover of the wagon poured down into it. There was nothing to do but remain in bed in the wet sheets until morning.

The next day the sun came out bright and hot. Nora hung the bedclothes on the thorn bushes, and everything dried out for the following night.

With soldiers in captivity, the sole defense of the country rested upon the settlers who had fled to Bulawayo for safety. Unfortunately they were untrained and unprofessional. In the darkness of the night, enemy campfires could be seen in a semicircle around the town. What kept them from attacking, nobody knew until later, when the Matabeles told how they had made many excursions into the city around two o'clock in the morning. They had climbed over the barbed-wire fences and entanglements in front of the machine guns around town, stepped over the sleeping forms of the English women and children who had gathered in the market square together for safety, and had walked by the sleeping husbands of these same women—supposedly on guard. Seeing the entire town so deep in slumber, the Matabeles had returned to their camps and advised that no attack be made. They were sure the white men were depending on witchcraft or some supernatural power; otherwise they would never all to go sleep so soundly in the face of danger.

Every night the missionaries had worship together, and Harry replaced his Bible in its box beside his bed. One morning he discovered to his dismay that the white ants had eaten all the gilt off the edges of the Bible and then cut one side of the back entirely off! "I should have known better," he chided himself, remembering how on one of his trips to the villages he had taken off his trousers and hung them on the limb of a tree before going to sleep. During the night the wind had blown them to the ground, and in the morning he had found that one leg had been eaten off up to the middle of the thigh. He had worn the strange-looking pants anyway, as they were the only ones he had with him on the trip.

Through January of 1896 the war continued, and the missionaries tried to make the best of their grim situation and cramped wagon home. From time to time, under the cover of night, Harry or Byron would sneak past enemy lines to check on the mission and return with corn, peanuts, chickens, beans, eggs, and pumpkins from the friendly people around the mission. And each time, they also brought the good news that their homes were still intact. But they were running out of money!

One day when their provisions were running low again, Harry decided it was his turn to take the risk of walking to the farm. While there, the natives told him that he could buy provisions at Chief Solusi's village, about four miles away. He bought the things he needed from the gracious chief and started back to the mission for the night.

As the sun was going down, Harry heard a voice say to him, "Get out of here quickly, for you are in danger."

Harry did not know where the danger might come from or who was speaking to him, but obediently, he hurried down the path as fast as he could run. He was afraid to sleep in the mission house that night, so he took his blankets and slept in the thick bush about half a mile away.

The next morning some friendly natives came up to the house and asked what path Harry had taken on the way home from Solusi's village the night before. When Harry told them, they looked at each other in astonishment and asked if he had seen any of the rebels.

"No, I didn't," Harry said, shaking his head.

"Where were you when the sun went down?" the natives asked.

"By the river," Harry replied. And then he learned that within a few minutes after he had heard the warning voice, about 300 of the rebels came down another trail and turned into the very one Harry had been on, headed the way Harry had just come from Solusi's village. They had heard Harry was there and had planned to kill him. If Harry had not run toward the mission when he heard the voice, he would no doubt have met the mob of rebels where the two trails met.

Though the missionaries were fortunate to be able to sneak out of town to the mission for food from time to time, they ate mostly cornmeal mush and perhaps a piece of fruit that the men had been able to pick from the trees outside of town at the risk of their lives.

On one of their escapades, the men were successful in buying some sacks of corn that some friendly villagers had raided from the rebels. By reselling the corn at the Bulawayo market, they made a rather large profit to add to their piggybank.

Among other things the natives raided and sold to the missionaries were some donkeys. Harry was thrilled with the new means of transportation! "I needn't be exhausted when I arrive in Bulawayo, if I can make the trip by donkey," he said to himself. "Besides, the trip will be considerably shorter than the six hours it takes to go on foot." But his jubilation evaporated that very day.

He started back happily from Bulawayo on the donkey, accompanied by an African boy on foot. All went well as they plodded through the darkness until they neared a rebel camp. Suddenly the donkey stuck up its nose and gave a terrific bray, making the hair on Harry's head stand up straight. He tried to quiet the animal by patting its neck, while his heart pounded wildly in his chest. He hoped the rebels didn't hear the donkey.

Harry toyed with the idea of getting off the donkey, but decided not to. And then, within sight of the rebel campfires, the donkey again stopped and uttered another heart-stopping bray.

Determined to take no more chances, Harry slipped off the animal, handed the reins to the native boy, and glided the rest of the way through the jungle to Bulawayo on his own legs.

Though Nora tried to bear their hardships cheerfully, the day came when she was seized by an irresistible craving for canned pears.

"If I could just taste the cool sweetness of a pear, I should be able to go on eating cornmeal," she told Harry.

"I don't know. We don't have much money," Harry reminded her. "But since I haven't spoiled you much lately, I shall now. Tomorrow morning I shall go to the government store and purchase for you a can of pears—whatever the price!"

And he did.

Chapter 8
A Boy Called "Mouth"

The missionaries were stuck in Bulawayo for six long months, six months of continual worry and illness and discomfort. Harry found himself frustrated that they had already been in the country for over a year, but half of that time he had been a captive under the wagon, without accomplishing the purpose for which he had been sent.

But at last, on September 5, 1896, the English declared victory. In order to achieve it they had burned native huts and destroyed their gardens. In desperate need of food, the Matabeles had surrendered. But the victory was not won without a price. During the rebellion, 150 English men, women, and children, had been brutally murdered, their houses burned by the natives.

The missionaries returned to the mission. What a happy sight greeted their eyes when they saw that their homes still stood! Only their garden, choked with weeds, saddened their hearts. They dug up their belongings, rejoicing that no damage had been done. Umlevu, the local chief, showed them a cave where he had stored the things he had found in their houses after their sudden departure.

As the missionaries set about moving back into their houses, a new problem faced them—the local inhabitants were starving. Here and there around the mission station, the missionaries found the skeletons of some natives that had starved to death.

It seemed that the people would eat any meat they could find, no matter how decayed it was. Sometimes on his travels among the villages, Harry's carriers would notice a vulture sitting on a tree near the path. Immediately they would put down their loads and run to see if any of the carcass on which the vultures had been feeding was left. If there was, the vultures got no more.

One day Harry noticed a man making off with one of his chickens. He decided to follow the man down the trail. As he was hurrying along he heard the cries of a child. He kept looking and listened, but could see no one. The cries seemed to be coming from underneath his feet. Looking down he discovered a child that had been thrust down an anteater hole and covered over with brush. The child was about three years of age. Pulling away the brush, Harry grasped the boy by the feet and drew him out. It looked as if he had been struck in the side of the face with an ax. The wound had festered and was filled with maggots. Finding out who the boy's mother was, Harry returned him to her and asked her what had happened. She said that the child had been crying for food for three days and she had none to give him. When she could stand listening to him no longer, she struck him with an ax, shoved him down the anteater hole, stopped her ears and ran. She thought he would die soon.

This is heathenism, Harry said to himself. These people need the good news about Christ so badly!

One day a little fellow named Malomo (mouth) was brought to the mission. The poor boy was mere skin and bones and scarcely able to walk. He was a slave, and his master demanded three sacks of grain for him. Harry told the master that he could not buy the slave, but he must set him free and leave him with them to care for. The master argued with Harry for over an hour. But he finally left the mission station, and the boy stayed with the Andersons.

Several months later, when Malomo was beginning to recover his strength, he stole some crackers and hid them away under the blanket of his bed.

One night while the boy was away at the mission worship gathering, Harry went into his bedroom for something and accidentally caught his toe under the edge of the blanket, turning the blanket back. And there he discovered the crackers stashed away.

When Malomo returned from worship, Harry took him outside for a walk. He put his arm around him and told him that Jesus was coming again soon to take His children home to His "village." Opening his Bible, Harry read to Malomo about the class of people who will remain outside the gates of God's village. Among those mentioned are thieves. Then, very gently, Harry showed him the box of crackers he had found under the boy's blanket.

With tears in his eyes, the little fellow grasped Harry's hand and said, "Father, I will never steal again." Then, choking down a sob, he added, "But I was so hungry!"

Together, they prayed that God would strengthen the boy to be true to His commandments.

The local people began bringing children to the missionaries to save them from starvation. As soon as the children were accepted, they had to have a bath. For many of them it was their first bath. At first they were petrified of the metal tub of water, but it didn't take long for them to relish splashing in it. And what a difference it made in their appearance when the dust was washed off their brown bodies and out of their hair!

They soon looked forward to their Friday afternoon baths and the special clothes they wore to church, which they called their "holy clothes." In time, thirty orphaned children lived at the mission, and a special house was built for them.

"Do you know what touches me the most about these children?" Nora commented one day as she and Mrs. Tripp sewed clothes for them. "We have never taught them to thank us for their meals, yet at the close of each meal, before they leave the table, they always say, 'Thank you.'

"The other day Harry had to leave the table before the children finished. One of the children took time to find him in the garden to tell him, 'Thank you'!"

The rainy season was soon upon the missionaries again. It was time to plant the garden. Since all of their oxen were dead, their plow was useless. But the little orphaned children worked together to chop up the weeds that had grown during the months of the war and helped plant a new crop of corn. During the heat of the day the missionaries gathered the children into the school for Bible lessons. The teacher said, "Your textbook is going to be your Bible. Your songbook is going to teach you English." They learned to write by marking in sand.

"I'm glad they don't know how much better equipped a real school is," Harry wrote back home.

When the day's work was over, Harry found his way to the cozy little home he and Nora had made and smiled when he thought of all God had brought them through. "During the heat of the war, I wondered if we would ever get another chance to really be missionaries," he told Nora one evening. "But look how everything has worked out! Instead of having to venture into the villages and hope the natives come to our Bible classes, we are now able to give them a better Christian example by having them live with us. And all this because of the war."

"No matter how hard Satan tries to discourage us, God can use whatever comes to His advantage, can't He?" Nora agreed with a smile.

Chapter 9
Death Comes to the Mission

In September, 1897, new missionaries, Mr. and Mrs. F. B. Armitage and their baby daughter, Violet, came to join the little group. They found the other missionaries busy making bricks in the hope of building houses that would provide better shelter than the ones made of mud. But though the bricks were already made, none of the missionaries was experienced in bricklaying.

"Well, actually, I've done quite a bit of bricklaying," Mr. Armitage admitted, and under his experienced eye, three new brick homes were built.

Each missionary's yard was 150 feet square, enclosed by a brick wall, with the house in the middle. Around each house was a covered porch, called a veranda, shaded by flowering bougainvillea vines. Orange, lemon and banana trees were planted in the spacious yards, along with shade trees and bushes similar to lilacs. On cool evenings, after a busy day of visiting villages and teaching the African women to sew, cook, and keep their huts clean, Nora often relaxed on her porch and enjoyed the sweet evening air, pungent with the perfume of flowers.

She was thankful for the helpers who shared her tasks of keeping the home running smoothly. It had not been hard to find a cook; the native boys were most eager to help, for they thoroughly enjoyed the treat of licking the plates and silverware after each meal. Nora asked them to wash the dinnerware in water and soap, but she was often too busy to check up on it and found that the best way to enjoy her next meal was to assume the dinnerware *had* been washed!

Harry called in a number of the chiefs of the district to show them his new brick house, asking them why they did not build better houses.

One old chief said, "Yes, your new house will be very comfortable; but think of the loss of time and labor if someone should die in it and it would have to be pulled down and destroyed."

To prevent this, the natives often carried a sick person outside of the village and let him die alone in the bush rather than in a house, because, according to their custom, a house in which anyone dies must be destroyed.

The missionaries enjoyed their new houses. They were happy. Then came the year 1898, and with it, a dreadful plague of malaria. In February, Dr. Carmichael became sick. Nora and Harry took him into their home to care for him.

Nora watched helplessly as his tortured body shook violently with chills, great beads of sweat drenching his sagging, lined face. He was losing weight at an alarming rate. Nora sat faithfully beside his bed, changing the cool cloths on his forehead and offering soothing words of comfort. He would often clasp his arm to his middle and writhe in pain as diarrhea cramps shot through him.

On the last day of February, Dr. Carmichael was delirious and soon slipped into a coma.

"How's he doing?" Harry asked when he came in from checking on the Tripps. Byron had been complaining of fatigue, but had refused to go to Cape Town on vacation.

"He's not responding," said Nora quietly. She gazed with fondness at the lined face of the man who had cared for them through other sicknesses. He was like a father to them all. He had always been the one who had cared for *them,* making *them* better. Now he was helpless against this wretched disease.

As they watched, the lined face suddenly relaxed, the chest lay still, and Dr. Carmichael's misery was over.

With a cry, Nora rushed to him. "He's gone!" she cried.

They buried him under one of the spreading trees on the compound, covering the grave with cement to protect it from wild animals, and placed a large tombstone there to mark his resting place.

The day after the funeral, Byron began to give in to the illness which his body had been valiantly resisting.

Nora and Harry now took in the Sparrows and their two sons who were also suffering from malaria. Mrs. Armitage took the Sparrows' two-year-old daughter, Amy, into her home to care for her.

Harry checked on the other families frequently. He made very few trips to the villages; it was his fellow missionaries who needed him now. One day he called Nora aside. "Baby Amy died early this morning," he said huskily. He pressed his eyes shut to stop the stinging tears.

"Oh, Harry—no!" Nora cried, throwing herself into his arms. "She was such a strong little cherub all during the war; and now she succumbs to malaria?" They sobbed together quietly, and then Nora asked, "Will you tell her parents?"

Amy was buried beside Dr. Carmichael in a tiny grave, her parents too ill to attend the funeral service.

Byron Tripp died that afternoon. At his funeral service, Harry remembered that it had been exactly three years to the day that the Tripps had first received the call to work in Africa.

"Everything costs something," Harry reminded the tiny group of mourners. He continued: "Everything is paid for not only in money, but also by someone's thought and care and toil. Our being in the world, able to enjoy its beauties and have a part in its work, has been paid for—and the price was a high one too. Pain, in the first place, and years of unceasing care and love and service have brought us where we are today—love and service that we can never repay except as we pass them on to others."

He looked into the faces of Mrs. Tripp and young George, searching for words of comfort for them. "Our hope of life beyond the grave, a life that shall never end, was bought with a price—the highest that could be paid in earth or heaven. What did it cost the Saviour to buy salvation for this rebellious and lost race, of which we, as truly as the heathen in Africa, are a part?

"We are told that 'the reflection of Christ's own character in

His people is His reward, and will be His joy throughout eternity.' Certainly Christ's own character was reflected in the life of our loved one, Elder Tripp."

Twelve-year-old George Tripp was the next to come down with malaria. "Mommy, am I going to die?" he moaned as he thrashed in his bed, chilling and sweating as the others had done.

"Elder Anderson has sent for a doctor," his mother assured him. "He'll be here soon."

George drifted in and out of consciousness, only half aware of Dr. Replogle's presence. His mother remained at his side. But in spite of the doctor's care, George died on April 4, 1898. On his tombstone were chiseled the words, "a youthful sacrifice."

Mrs. Armitage was the next to die, leaving her husband alone with baby Violet. In the short span of two months, five of the missionaries were dead. The somber few that remained encouraged each other and renewed their commitment to serve God, no matter what the cost. They thanked God that they had the promise of a better life in heaven with not only their immediate families, but the people with whom they had shared the promises of God.

It was several weeks before they returned to their regular duties of working for the Africans. To fill her days, Mrs. Tripp took care of baby Violet for Mr. Armitage while he visited in the villages.

In time, Mrs. Tripp and Mr. Armitage discovered that they enjoyed being together. Romance was not dead in the mission field; and after a suitable amount of time, Mr. Armitage invited Mrs. Tripp to share his mission career. It was an invitation she gladly accepted. They were married shortly thereafter, and she became a loving stepmother to baby Violet. Together, Mr. and Mrs. Armitage worked in Africa for 20 more years.

Chapter 10
African Ways—and Wisdom

The year 1899 was a joyous one for the missionaries, especially the Andersons. On March 25, in the care of doctors in Bulawayo, Nora gave birth to a baby daughter whom they named Naomi, after Nora's mother. It was harder now for Harry to leave home on his travels to the villages, but still he carried on.

On December 1, 1901, five and a half years after coming to Africa, the missionaries held their first baptism. It was a day of rejoicing for all of them. Now that there were native Christian teachers at Solusi, Harry and Nora decided to homestead again in another area in need of a mission station.

Harry felt they should move somewhere in Barotseland, and he set out alone with a group of native boys to find some land to buy for a new school. On that trip he passed by Victoria Falls, visiting the grave of David Livingstone, the man whose life had first inspired Harry to go to Africa. It was a trip marked by highs and lows. A few days after visiting David Livingstone's grave, one of Harry's carriers walked off with the group's entire food pack of dried food! They never found him.

Near an African village that night, Harry shot a deer and offered the hindquarters to the village chief in exchange for some corn. The chief agreed and called his women together to pound the corn into cornmeal, from which the carriers made their supper.

Harry and his group made their camp within the village stockade, but away from the filth and noise near the huts. He was so tired that evening, he could hardly stay awake to eat his supper. About midnight, one of Harry's boys shook him awake with an alarmed whispered message. *"Mfundisi*, get up quickly!" he said. "They are going to kill us and you too!" Harry rubbed his eyes and sat up suddenly. The steady throbbing of a deep-toned drum quickened his pulse. In the middle of the village, around a blazing fire, the men of the village were involved in a frenzied war dance, shaking their spears at the fire and screaming out their war cries.

Harry hurried to the chief's house and asked him to come out and talk to him. The chief refused. But even if he had come out, they would have had a hard time communicating, because Harry did not understand his language. However, he found a translator and discovered that the chief was upset because his women had not been paid for the cornmeal they pounded out. "The meat was your payment," Harry said, but the chief said, "No; the meat was a gift." Harry asked where the meat was, and the chief said it was in his hut. Dropping to his knees, Harry crawled into the chief's hut and felt around in the darkness. He found the meat and took it to the women's hut and threw it in the door. Then he went to the edge of the village and began to roll up his bedding.

The chief sent messengers to warn Harry that if he left the village now, in the middle of the night, the lions would get him. "Better to be eaten by lions that be killed by dogs," Harry returned. This shamed the chief, for hospitality to visitors is a strict code in Africa. He promised Harry that he would do him no harm for the rest of the night.

So Harry slept a few more hours in the village, the boy who first awakened him insisting he would stay on guard. There was no further trouble that night, but they left very early the next morning.

As always, finding good drinking water was a major problem. At one point, after trekking through deep sand from daybreak until two in the afternoon, Harry's little group of carriers came upon some stagnant pools of water covered with green slime—but at least it was water, and it was wet! Without taking the usual precaution of boiling it, Harry lay down on the ground, scraped the scum to the side, and drank all he wanted.

A short time later, he came down with diarrhea. Alone in the wilderness without doctors or medical care, and without proper food and shelter, Harry was sure he was going to die. The native boys did what they could to make him comfortable, but they didn't have much to work with.

One evening, when his strength was at its lowest ebb, Harry called the native helpers around him and told them he did not think he would live through the night. Directing them to a large thorn tree close by, he told them to dig his grave there, sew his body in blankets and bury it. "And tell my wife that I loved her and the baby till the end. Also, tell the workers at the mission not to abandon the work in this country just because I have died. My grave at the side of the road will mark their way into this new territory." Then, totally exhausted, he laid his head back down on his pillows to rest. He closed his eyes and dozed off into what he thought would be his last sleep.

He slept soundly all night long.

In the morning, he awoke to find he was still alive. Soon a native man came into their camp and said there was a white man about eight miles from where they were! Harry's boys constructed a stretcher and carried him to the white man's house, where he stayed for two weeks until he regained his strength. Then he continued on his trip to the villages.

Harry learned from the Africans about as much as he taught them. At one point of their trip they had to cross a wide river. Harry started taking off his shoes and socks and rolling up his pant legs before he started across. "You go ahead and swim across with our food, and I'll follow you," Harry told the men who were with him.

"No. There are crocodiles in the river!" they said in alarm.

"They haven't had time to come up into these rivers this year," Harry responded, knowing that the crocodiles always came at the start of the rainy season. "But if you're afraid, then I will go first."

The natives grabbed his arms, hanging on him and begging him not to go into the river. The whites of their eyes shone with fear in their dark faces.

Balancing on one leg, Harry continued stripping his legs and feet of clothing. "Let go of me, please," Harry requested. "I have to find a place to set up a mission station."

"Please wait a few minutes before you go in," the boys pleaded. One of them ran along the bank until he found a stone as large as Harry's head and tossed it into the middle of the river.

Harry watched patiently, his arms crossed over his chest, sure that nothing would happen. To his surprise, as soon as the stone hit the water, three crocodiles put up their noses.

"You see what would have happened if you have gone in, instead of the stone?" the boys said smugly.

"Well!" Harry replied sheepishly, "I guess we can't cross here." He went upriver to a place where the river was only ankle deep, and the entire troupe crossed without incident.

At last Harry came to a spring about which he had heard. The water was sweet and cool—a pleasing contrast to the flat taste of warm, boiled water they had to drink at Solusi. The area was forested on one side, with a rise overlooking a gulley, which would become a river during the rainy season. It seemed like the perfect place for the home Harry planned for Nora.

With a light heart, Harry pounded wooden stakes into the ground around the spring to claim the land and he gave the native chief who owned the land an English pound as a down payment. Then he returned home to Solusi, eager to tell Nora about the beautiful new place he had found for them.

Chapter 11
Lions in the Bush

Harry and Nora returned to America in 1905 on furlough. The Andersons spent eight months in America, visiting churches and telling stories of their struggles and joys in Africa. They asked for money so they could buy land for the new school in Barotseland, and the people gave generously. Then back across the Atlantic the Andersons went, to England and then Cape Town. From there they boarded the train as they had the first time, but now the rails went all the way to Bulawayo, saving them several weeks' travel by oxcart.

But this trip would not be without an oxcart journey. After packing up their things at Solusi, Harry and Nora and six-year-old Naomi began their wagon journey toward the beautiful spot Harry had picked out in Barotseland. It was a dangerous region, infested with lions. Sometimes the lions appeared even in daylight.

One morning, as the helpers were yoking up the oxen, Harry heard a commotion in some tall grass ahead of the wagon and caught sight of what he thought was a spotted hyena, one of the most cowardly and despised animals in the bush. The oxen had been nicely lined up for the start, when they suddenly stampeded back and crowded around the wagon. Harry instructed the helpers to get the oxen straightened out quickly so they could continue their journey.

The lead boy protested. "*Mfundisi*," he said, using a respectful form of address, "I think there is a lion in the path. You should drive him away with your gun."

"That's not a lion; it's only a spotted hyena," Harry replied. "I saw it myself just a few moments ago."

The driver gave Harry a disbelieving look as he straightened out the oxen again, muttering that he had never seen the animals act like that when all they smelled was a hyena.

All seemed ready again when suddenly the oxen rushed back around the wagon, much to Harry's annoyance. Again the driver declared that there was a lion in the path. Again Harry assured him it was only a hyena.

Suddenly, from the tall grass in front of the wagon came a tremendous roar. The Africans looked at Harry and asked with a trace of irony if he had ever heard a hyena roar like that! Harry grinned, but said nothing as he fired a couple of shots into the grass. The lion took the hint and disappeared, and the safari continued.

No road led through that wild country—not even a trail. When the travelers came to streams without bridges, Harry and his helpers often had to scout up and down the bank, seeking a ford sufficiently shallow to let them cross. In other places they encountered trees so thick that they had to clear them away with axes.

One Friday night the travelers made their beds as usual on the ground. The oxen seemed unusually restless, pulling and pushing against the wagon tongue. Early the next morning when the boys were taking the animals out to graze, Harry heard exclamations of surprise and asked what was the matter.

"Come and see!" the boys exclaimed. "Lions are here!"

Harry hurried over to take a look. Sure enough, there in the sand all around the camp were tracks which told a startling story. Three lions had passed right near their camp. Less than fifteen feet from the spot where Harry and Nora and little Naomi slept peacefully, a lion had stopped and looked, and then moved on. "Surely the 'angel of the Lord' surrounded us last night," Harry said reverently.

The next day the carts rolled past the wooden pegs marking the property Harry had staked out several years before and arrived on the land where they would build their new home. They camped near the sweet springs on a forested hill that overlooked the creek. Nora breathed in the clean air and smiled.

"It's so lovely here," she said, "I can't wait until we build our new home."

"I plan to do that first thing, before I even start going out to look for students," Harry assured her.

Two days later, while Harry was in the woods chopping down trees for their new home, a young native boy came up to him and said he had come to attend school.

"But there isn't a school yet," Harry informed him. "There isn't even a house for a teacher!"

"Oh, but word has gone out to all the villages that you are a teacher, and I have come to school!" With that, the boy sat down against a tree to wait, silently watching Harry work.

Harry talked it over with Nora that evening around a smoky campfire. "Would Jesus turn him away?" Nora wondered; and Harry had to agree that He wouldn't. So the next evening Harry and the boy began schoolwork by learning each other's language.

The next day five more boys came to "school." At the end of a month there were forty boys in school, whose willing hands helped build a house for the Andersons as well as dormitories and classrooms for themselves. Some of the boys had walked as much as 500 miles to go to school!

Chapter 12
Goodbye, Nora

After the school was established, Harry again began making trips to outlying villages to share the Bible. As always, he went on foot.

While Nora was glad that he could share the gospel with the Africans, she often suffered from recurring bouts of malaria and found it difficult to care for Naomi when she was so ill. During one of Harry's trips in 1907, Nora felt the symptoms of the disease coming on. She dosed herself with quinine and went on with her chores as best she could. But when Harry came home, she fell into his arms and said, "I feel so weak, Harry. I'm so glad you're home."

That night she awakened Harry and said, "I'm chilly; are you?"

"No. Let me get you a hot-water bottle," he offered. He placed hot, wrapped bricks and hot-water bottles around her, but they seemed to do little good. She shook violently for an hour and a half, her teeth chattering loudly, great beads of sweat drenching her face. Watching her, Harry knew she had the dreaded blackwater fever, a usually fatal type of malaria. He sat beside her bed throughout the weekend without sleeping. He refused to leave her side. As he watched her tortured body, he ached for her. She had always been the love of his life. What would he do without her?

Sunday night he noticed with alarm that her heart was skipping beats. He placed cold cloths on her chest in an effort to shock her heart and keep it beating. It would beat once, twice, and stop, and he worried that it wouldn't start again. The closest doctor was a hundred miles away.

Sensing that Nora's life was drawing to a close, Harry took Naomi gently by the hand and led her to her mother's bed. Nora was unconscious. Harry held his little daughter in his arms and whispered quietly, "My darling, I am sorry to tell you that I do not know whether Mama will wake up when you do in the morning."

Naomi studied her mother's pale face quietly, brushing the back of her hand against her cheeks as the tears fell silently. Then she turned and left the room. Harry heard her quiet voice in her room pleading with God to spare her mother's life. And God heard that prayer!

The next morning Nora was still alive, though still very sick. Desperate to get her to a doctor, Harry wrapped her in a hammock and called on two of the natives to assist him in tying the hammock to two long poles. They carried Nora two and a half miles through the forest to the point where the railway lines bordered the mission property. Naomi stumbled along as fast as her short legs would carry her, without complaint.

They waited all day for a train to come by. Day turned into night. At last, in the early hours of Tuesday morning, Harry heard the rumble of the approaching train. He stood in the middle of the tracks swinging his lantern and then stepped aside as the engineer stopped the train. The little family and Nora traveled to the town of Kimberly, several hours away, where friends and medical care awaited them.

By Tuesday of the next week, Nora was feeling better, and Wednesday morning she called Harry into her room. Her dark eyes were sunken in her pale face, a long, dark braid over her shoulder the only color against the pillow. Her arms, covered by the long sleeves of her cotton nightgown lay clasped on top of the dark, homemade quilt covering her. Harry hurried to her side and stroked her arm.

Nora managed a weak smile. "Harry, I want you to take that train tonight and go back to the mission," she said.

"I can't do that," Harry said at once, brushing a curl off her forehead.

"But you must go back," Nora said softly.

"Nora," Harry said, taking her small hand in his own and stroking it gently. "Do you remember the day we were married? I promised you I would stay with you until death parted us. I can't leave you now, when you need me!"

"But I don't need you now," she replied gently. "I'm feeling better, and I have good doctors here. They'll take care of me." She searched his eyes for a sign of agreement, but saw none. When Harry made up his mind, there was no changing it. But there were so many others who needed his strength more than she did. "The mission needs you more," Nora said. "There are those sheep of ours. There are those boys and girls we have gathered to the mission station. Who will take care of them?"

Harry rose and walked to the window, his hand on the back of his neck, massaging his tight muscles as he considered Nora's request. He stared out the window for a long moment with a deep sigh, and then turned to face her.

"I can't leave," he stated, almost helplessly. He strode over to her bed and sat down. His voice was soft. "I love you, Nora. I love you too much to leave you and Naomi here alone. Especially now."

With all the strength she could muster, Nora raised herself up onto her elbow. Looking straight into Harry's eyes, she whispered as resolutely as she could, "Harry, you have to do it."

With a cry, Harry took her in his arms and held her. They clung to each other silently for several minutes. Then he kissed her and left the room to pack up his things. He would go. Then, with a heavy heart, Harry kissed Naomi goodbye and took the train back home.

Nora was moved to a hospital in Cape Town, and for the next month she seemed to improve. She wrote to Harry about the little garden she wanted to start near the house with rosebushes which would remind her of America, the country she had left behind. Harry looked forward to her return. But one morning the messenger boy ran across the mission yard to Harry's house with a letter and two telegrams.

Suddenly gripped by icy fingers of fear, Harry tore open the first telegram. "Your wife has had a relapse of blackwater fever," it said. Harry groaned and tore open the next telegram more fearfully. "Your wife passed away yesterday with the blackwater fever. Buried this afternoon. Sorry."

At last, with shaking hands, Harry opened the letter from Nora. She had dictated it to one of the nurses before she died. "My darling Harry," it said. "I know I am not going to make it through this attack of the fever. Take good care of Naomi. Stay by the mission, and make it all we have planned, under God, it should be. In a little while we're going home."

Harry fell into the nearest chair, too stunned to cry.

Chapter 13
A New Mrs. Anderson and Other Stories

Harry sent a telegram to Solusi asking for a replacement teacher to substitute for him, and when a replacement came, he went to Cape Town to be with Naomi, talk to Nora's doctor, and visit her grave. Then he returned to the Barotseland mission with Naomi.

In 1910 Harry and eleven-year-old Naomi returned to America on furlough. Naomi was able to attend church school for the first time in her life and was so happy to have other little girls to play with. While in Washington, D.C., Harry met a young woman named Mary Perrin, and before the furlough was over, Harry and Mary were married.

No sooner had they returned to Africa than Mary was struck with recurring bouts of malaria, often burning up with fever. Harry stayed by her side when he was home, worrying that he would have to bury her himself as well as preach the funeral sermon. But through it all, she shared Harry's commitment to mission service, and her only regret when she was sick was that she could not go out into the villages and help the natives. Mary survived and with Harry continued to give many more years of faithful service. It was during this time that Harry took the visiting Elder Porter on the lion hunt.

The droughts came again. In 1916, neither the mission gardens nor those of the villagers grew under the scorching sun. The earth became parched and cracked, splitting into pieces like jigsaw puzzles for miles.

The natives did their best to make the rain fall, visiting the graves of their ancestors, crying for rain, but all to no avail.

One day, as the natives passed through the mission compound on their way to plead at their ancestors' graves, they were asked by one of the teachers why they did not pray to God if they wanted rain. "Your chief is a dead man and cannot hear you," the teacher said. "None of your singing, dancing, or crying does any good, for you are praying to a dead man!"

"We'll see," the natives replied. "We will go to the grave of our old chief today and ask for rain, and you go to your God and we'll see who gets the rain."

After breakfast that morning, the teacher called all the students into the church for a prayer meeting. They read the story of Elijah on Mount Carmel who prayed for rain, and then they spent the next hours until lunch, pleading with God to do the same miracle again, to demonstrate to the heathen that He was, indeed, the true God.

That afternoon a cloud came up from the east, passed over the school cornfield, and gave it a good watering. It went on to the west about two miles, but stopped before reaching the gardens of the natives. Then it turned back, and a second shower fell upon the school's gardens.

That evening, when the natives returned from their chief's grave, the mission cornfield was too wet to cultivate, while their own, which lay just across the river, had scarcely received a drop. They were speechless. Later, when a plague of illness swept through the village, the witch doctor consulted his rhinoceros and elephant bones and "learned" that the illness had come because the villagers were not attending Sabbath School and church at the mission. They soon began attending regularly!

By now Harry and Mary had been in Africa nearly six years. Though he didn't want to admit it, Harry's health was failing, and his body needed a rest. Naomi, a young girl of seventeen, needed to spend some time with young people of her own country. So the Andersons went on furlough that year. Because World War I was going on at the time and ships were being sunk at an alarming rate, Harry and Mary were advised to stay in America for a couple of years, until the next General Conference Session.

They stayed for two and a half years until 1919. When they left, Naomi bade them a sad farewell. She would stay in America to pursue a college education. "But as soon as I am finished," she told her father, smiling through her tears, "I'm going to be a missionary to Africa too."

During his next term of service Harry bought a 1923 Model T Ford Pickup and learned to drive it. Unfortunately, he was not as handy with cars as he was with preaching; and on many trips, when the car broke down, he didn't know how to fix it.

Since there were no gas stations in the jungles, they had to carry fuel tanks strapped to the outside of the car, and this presented hazards of its own.

On one journey, which Mary would say was the most eventful day of the thirty-five years she spent in mission work, a lioness suddenly appeared in the middle of the road, sitting like a dog on its haunches. It was early morning. Harry blew the horn of his car, but the lioness didn't budge.

He decided to drive straight toward the lioness, gunning the motor loudly. When the pickup came to within ten feet of the lioness, she leaped into the grass.

As they passed between two flat-topped hills, they rounded a sharp corner and were startled to see another car approaching them at top speed. Neither driver had expected to meet the other. Both swerved, narrowly missing each other. The near accident happened so fast there was no time to slow down. The little pickup kept right on bumping down the road.

Harry had been told that the road he should take to Elizabethville was a new one, so when he saw a new wide road taking off into the forest, he turned onto it. Other tire tracks were visible in the dust.

Suddenly the travelers saw a giant cobra just by the side of the road. It was probably ten to twelve feet long, its body as thick as a man's arm. The snake's body was coiled, with its head perhaps five feet above the ground. It swayed angrily back and forth, prepared to strike. There was no time to dodge. The African boy sitting on the running board screamed. As the pickup roared past, the cobra struck at the boy but missed and hit the fender instead with a noise that sounded like a steel hammer. The boy shrieked again, this time in relief. Had the snake struck him, he would have been dead in a few minutes.

"What next!" Mary gasped. "First a lion, then a near collision, and now a cobra." But there was more.

After about ten miles, the road ended abruptly. They had taken the wrong road. Harry turned the truck around, and they hurried back the way they had just come. He hoped they could still make it to Elizabethville before dark, since cataracts were beginning to impair his night vision.

When they got back to the road they had first been on, they stopped to consider which way to go. As they stood there, they all became aware of a roaring sound in the distance. It wasn't any animal. Harry sniffed the air and looked up and saw wisps of smoke drifting over the tops of the trees toward them. It was an advancing forest fire.

"Get in the truck! Quick!" Harry called. "We've got to get out of here!"

Hoping to avoid the worst of the fire, he turned the pickup onto the road leading to the right. Tall grass which had grown up in the abandoned road made fast driving impossible, for any clump might hide an anthill. Harry had seen more than one car totally wrecked from running into one of those obstacles at high speed.

Soon they came to a place where the fire had recently passed. Many bushes in the middle of the road were still smoldering, but they couldn't turn back now. The passengers trembled as they saw sparks flying up all around the car. They hoped the gasoline they were carrying wouldn't explode. The native boy still clinging to the running board was unable to protect himself from the sparks, so Mary kept brushing sparks from his clothing as they rushed on.

At last they emerged onto a fine new road which led them safely through the forest. In the late afternoon they came to a large river. There was a steep incline they had to negotiate in order to get onto a ferry raft that waited at the bottom. Harry had heard of drivers who failed to brake in time and had shot right off the far end of the ferry raft into the river.

They made it onto the raft safely, but the current swept them downstream beyond the connecting road on the other bank, and it took the boatmen several hours to pole the raft upstream so they could continue their journey.

They reached Elizabethville about midnight and somehow found their way to the missionaries' house in the suburbs.

"We're late," Harry said, "but that's better than not getting here at all."

Chapter 14
The Rest of the Story

After the school in Barotseland was going well, Harry and Mary moved to Angola and homesteaded there as they began another new school. Between 1934 and 1944, Harry and Mary lived in relative ease in the flourishing city of Cape Town, where Harry served in the Division as superintendent of the schools he had founded. Although he was old enough to retire, Harry preferred to work. "They may put me on a shelf someday, but when they do, there will definitely be something moving on that shelf! " he said firmly. His work in Cape Town involved much travel, but Harry thrived on it. Mary kept busy at home teaching the Africans to be Bible workers.

In 1944, fifty years after the land had been donated for Solusi College, the school decided to hold a Golden Jubilee Celebration. As the hour of the celebration approached, hundreds of Africans and Europeans lined the road leading into the compound. Far down the road they saw a cloud of dust and heard the crack of a whip as a large wagon pulled by sixteen oxen rolled slowly toward the Solusi Mission. All eyes focused on the man with the white beard who was cracking the whip and urging the oxen on. Yes, it was none other than the hero of the occasion, William Harrison Anderson, reenacting the part he had played half a century before. He was now 74 years old and still going strong.

But whereas the earlier wagon had been driven onto a settlement of four tiny huts, he now drove onto a sprawling campus with long dormitories and classrooms, sidewalks, and roads leading to the faculty housing where comfortable brick dwellings stood, surrounded by trees. On the wagon rode Harry's wife, Mary, and another woman missionary dressed as pioneers.

The wagon drew up to the grandstand, and the missionary wives were escorted to seats of honor.

There were speeches and telegrams of congratulations from America and the local government, followed by three days of remembrances by the old missionaries and a visit to the cemetery to lay wreaths on the graves of those who had given their lives in mission service. Of the original families, Harry was the only one still living.

As he looked at the prospering college around him, Harry remembered the years when there were only grass huts and grassland; how the corn was devastated by the locusts not once, but many times; how they had had to leave their homes in time of war. But those memories only deepened his pleasure as he saw what the college had now become.

"I have given my money; my strength, my wife Nora, and I intend to give the rest of my poor self to finish the work God has given me to do," he said. "To quote the words of a song we sang nearly fifty years ago when we made the journey to this place, 'In a little while we *shall* be going home.'"

The evening before the Andersons were to leave Solusi, a knock came on the door of the home where they were visiting. Some people outside wished to see the old missionary. A group of about twenty gray-headed men and women had come to bid farewell to their friend. One woman stepped forward and presented an intricately handwoven basket to Elder Anderson. When he failed to recognize her, she told him she was an orphan he had saved during the terrible famine. Then another woman, who had also belonged to the same orphan group, presented a basket.

When Harry had graciously received their gifts, a man came up to him and said, "I am Malomo. My starving parents sold me to an African trader who tried to sell me to the missionary. You persuaded my master to give me to the mission. Do you remember that night when I stole some crackers and hid them under my blanket?" Harry nodded. "You might have sent me away, but you didn't. Instead, you prayed with me and taught me the right way."

"Malomo," Harry whispered happily. Then he clasped him in a friendly embrace. "And what have you done between then and now?" he asked.

"I am a preacher—like you," Malomo answered proudly. "I teach my people about the God of heaven who is coming soon to take all of us to His 'village,' where there is always enough food and water—and where the beasts are friendly."

"Oh, Malomo. I am so happy," Harry said. That suffering boy had become a powerful preacher for God.

Feelings of joy and sorrow mingled in Harry's heart as he gazed into the faces of those friends of long ago and bade them goodbye.

The next morning Harry Anderson and his wife left Solusi for the last time. He had given fifty years of his life in service to Africa.

Harry and Mary spent some time in India after that, and then in the Far East. At last, in 1948, when Harry was 78, he and Mary returned to America to live. Harry still burned with energy, getting up before sunrise each morning to begin the day. He died suddenly of a heart attack in 1950 at his home in Claremont, North Carolina. He had risen at 4:30 that morning to work in his garden before leaving on a speaking trip. He died in midsentence while shaving and chatting with Mary.

His was a name that would not be forgotten in the history of African missions. His life was based on answering one question: "Lord, what wilt Thou have me to do?" And it was his prayer that other young people would ask this same question too.